Snakes

by RUTH BELOV GROSS

SCHOLASTIC INC.

New York Toronto London Auckland Sydney

To my friends in the Allen Room

PHOTO CREDITS

K. Bobrowsky: cover, 8, 9, 10, 28, 46, 47, 52, 53; Brush/Monkmeyer: 21; Nathan W. Cohen: 29, 41, 42, 43; Field Museum of Natural History: 20; Jack Fields/Photo Researchers: 33; John H. Gerard/Monkmeyer: 14, 15; John H. Gerard/National Audubon Society: 6 left, 11, 59; Charles Hackenbrock: 19; Hal Harrison: 18; Robert C. Hermes/National Audubon Society: 25 right; Latham/Monkmeyer: 34; Norman R. Lightfoot/Photo Researchers: 39; William M. Partington/National Audubon Society: 56; Roy Pinney/Monkmeyer: 25 left; E. Hanumantha Rao/Photo Researchers: 60; Leonard Lee Rue III/Monkmeyer: 22, 30, 40, 48, 49; Robert S. Simmons: 54, 55; Alvin E. Staffan/National Audubon Society: 38, 51; Alvin E. Staffan/Photo Researchers: 45; Dade W. Thornton/National Audubon Society: 57, 58; Robert G. Tuck, J.: 6 right, 44, 50; Walker Van Riper/University of Colorado Museum: 17, 26.

ISBN: 0-590-41706-1

12 11 10 9 8 7 6 5 4 3   0 1 2/9

Printed in the U.S.A.   08

My warmest thanks to Bob Tuck, who encouraged me, helped me, and became my friend while I was writing this book. Bob Tuck was then president of the Maryland Herpetological Society and instructor in amphibians and reptiles, Smithsonian Associates. He is now Curator in Zoology, Department of Environmental Conservation, in Teheran.

I would also like to thank George Foley, Department of Herpetology, The American Museum of Natural History, for his help.

R. B. G.

A note from the author

There are about two thousand different kinds of snakes in the world. This book does not tell you about all of them. It does tell you about some of the most interesting snakes.

Mostly it is about the snakes that live in the United States and Canada.

Of all the snakes in the world, only a very few kinds are poisonous. Many snakes are useful to people. Farmers like to have some kinds of snakes around because the snakes eat mice and rats. And gardeners like the snakes that eat insects.

When you read this book you will find out about some poisonous snakes, and you will find out about many snakes that are not poisonous. When you have finished the book, you will know a lot of things about the way snakes live.

Contents

The snake on the cover is a *rough green snake.*

These little garter snakes are one day old. They are about seven inches long.

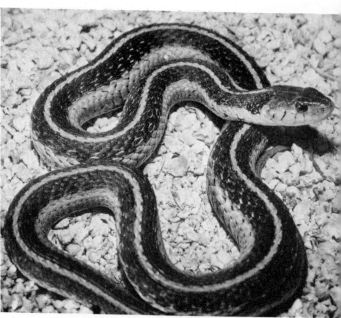

This garter snake is fully grown. It is about two feet long.

Mother corn snake laying her eggs

Baby corn snakes coming out
of their eggs

Most baby snakes stay inside their shells for two or three months.

These baby snakes are coming out of their shells. About half of the baby snakes are males. About half are females.

Each baby snake has a tiny tooth, called an egg tooth, right on the tip of its snout. When the little snake is ready to come out of its shell, it makes a hole in the shell with its egg tooth. Then it crawls out through the hole.

A few hours later, the egg tooth will fall off. The baby snake does not need it anymore.

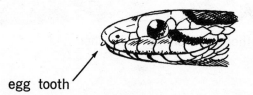
egg tooth

Some snakes do not lay eggs. They give birth to their babies.

Garter snakes usually have a lot of babies at one time. Other kinds of snakes have about 10 at a time. Some have two or three.

This mother garter snake has just given birth to her babies. In a few hours the little garter snakes will find something to eat — maybe some frogs or toads or earthworms.

There are 29 baby garter snakes in this picture. Most baby snakes are born in August or September.

All baby snakes can take care of themselves from the very first day of their lives.

Do the parent snakes do anything for their babies? No. There is nothing for them to do. Baby snakes do not need any help in getting food. And they do not need any help in protecting themselves from danger.

Most mother snakes go away as soon as they lay their eggs or give birth to their babies. The father snakes do not even stay that long. They go away as soon as they mate with the mother snakes.

Shedding

When a baby snake is still very young, something special happens. The outside part of its skin peels off.

We say that the snake is *shedding its skin*. But all that comes off is a thin outside layer.

A few months later, the snake sheds its skin again. It sheds again and again while it is growing up and after it is fully grown. Scientists think that shedding has something to do with a chemical that the snake makes in its body.

A snake always starts shedding at the head end. First it rubs its head against something rough. The rubbing helps to break the old skin around the snake's snout and chin.

In the first picture, a hog-nose snake has just started to shed. The old skin over its snout has already peeled off.

Instead of eyelids, a snake has a bit of clear, hard skin over each eye — something like the glass cover on a wrist watch. The snake can see right through this skin. It comes off with the rest.

In the second picture, the snake is halfway

out of its old skin. In the third picture, it is almost all the way out. The snake helps its skin come off by crawling slowly. The skin comes off inside out, the way your sweater does when you take it off.

In the last picture, the snake is wearing its new skin. It is brighter and shinier than the old skin. You can see the old skin lying on the ground near the snake.

Snake keepers can tell when a snake is getting ready to shed. A week or two before it sheds, a snake is likely to get mean and nasty. Usually it stops eating. Its colors are not as bright as they were. Its eyes turn a cloudy blue.

What is going on? The snake is making a new layer of skin under the old one.

What does a snake's skin feel like? A snake's skin is dry and smooth. Some people think that a snake's skin is slippery and slimy and wet. But they are wrong.

This king snake is eating a lizard.

Eating

When a snake has finished shedding, it is ready to eat again.

Most snakes eat whenever they can. They eat whether they need the food or not. A scientist once gave 30 tree frogs to a garter snake. The snake ate every single frog.

Many kinds of snakes eat other kinds of snakes. They never eat their own kind. This king snake is eating a garter snake.

All snakes eat animals. They eat them alive or right after they have been killed.

A snake does not chew its food. It swallows everything whole. It starts on one end of an animal and keeps swallowing until it gets the whole animal down. If the snake is eating a big animal, the meal may take an hour or more.

Snakes can eat big animals because snakes can open their mouths very wide.

When you open your mouth, your bottom jaw moves down. It moves down in the front but not in the back. When a snake opens its mouth, the bottom jaw moves down in the front *and* in the back. So a snake can open its mouth much wider than you can.

A snake's mouth can stretch until it is two or three times its usual size.

Different snakes eat different animals. They eat the ones that are easiest for them to catch and to swallow.

The easiest animal for a snake to swallow is a snake! Maybe that is why a lot of snakes eat other snakes.

Some snakes also eat eggs.

No snake will eat plants or flowers or fruits or vegetables.

This yellow rat snake is eating an egg.

Some of the animals that snakes eat

fish	rabbits	frogs
chickens	chipmunks	toads
mice	insects	lizards
rats	earthworms	salamanders
squirrels	birds	snakes

No snake will eat all of the animals on this list. Most snakes will eat three or four kinds of animals. A few snakes eat only one kind of animal.

This is an African rock python that has just eaten a whole goat.

A meal like this is enough to keep the python alive for a year. Most of the time, though, snakes do not eat such big meals.

Most zoos cannot keep a lot of live animals around for their snakes to eat. So zoos usually give their snakes dead animals instead. After a while the snakes learn to eat the zoo food.

Zoo keepers have even taught some snakes to eat strips of raw meat. They rub the raw meat with a mouse's skin first, to give it the right smell.

Snakes in the zoo are fed every week or so. But a snake that has to get its own food may not find anything to eat for months. A snake can live without food for a long time.

Big snakes can live without food for an *especially* long time. Once there was a python in a zoo that did not eat anything for three years. Then it began eating again.

Getting Food

How does a snake find something to eat? Sometimes it goes out hunting. And sometimes it stays where it is until something good to eat comes along.

A snake uses its eyes and nose to find the food. It also uses its tongue. The tongue helps the snake do a better job of smelling.

Every time a snake flicks out its tongue, it is checking the air for smells. Flick! The tongue shoots out. Quick! The tongue goes back in the snake's mouth. It brings back smells from the air outside.

If a frog is hopping by, the tongue brings back a froggy smell. And maybe the snake will have a froggy dinner.

A snake's tongue is long and narrow. We say it is *forked*, because it is split at the tip. Some people think that a snake can sting with its tongue, but no snake can do that.

The snake in the picture is a rattlesnake.

21

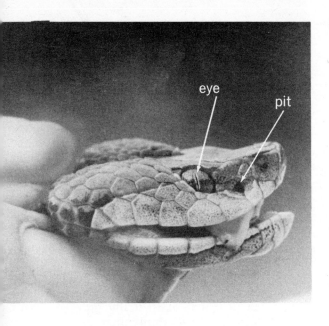

A rattlesnake has a pit on each side of its face.

Rattlesnakes, copperheads, and cottonmouths have an extra way of finding their food. They have holes, called *pits,* on their faces. One pit is near each eye.

When one of these snakes is near something warm, it feels the warmth with its pits. The pits help the snake find a warm animal in the dark.

Most pythons and some kinds of boas also have pits. These snakes usually have lots of pits around their lips.

Snakes can never find any food by listening. They do not have ears.

What is the first thing a snake does when it finds an animal to eat? It makes sure the animal does not get away!

Quick as a flash, the snake grabs the animal with its teeth. Then the snake may swallow the animal alive. The animal will die in the snake's stomach.

Some snakes eat all their food while it is still alive. These snakes eat only small, harmless animals — animals that will not give them any trouble.

Other snakes eat some of their food alive — the small, harmless animals. But they kill big animals and dangerous animals before eating them.

There are two ways that snakes can kill animals. One way is by squeezing. The other way is with poison. No snake can squeeze and use poison too.

A snake that squeezes is called a *constrictor*. Bull snakes, rat snakes, king snakes, and many others are constrictors.

After a constrictor grabs an animal with its teeth, it wraps itself around the animal. It squeezes the animal hard. In a minute or two the animal cannot breathe, and it dies.

When a poisonous snake grabs an animal, it sends poison into the animal's body. The poison comes out of extra-big teeth called *fangs*. In a few minutes the animal dies from the poison.

Many snakes have no way to kill animals before eating them.

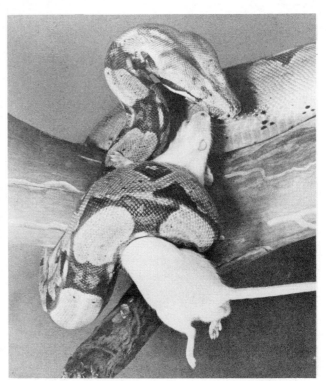

A garter snake is eating a frog while the frog is still alive. Garter snakes have no way of killing their food before they eat it. They eat animals that cannot fight back and hurt them.

This boa constrictor is squeezing a white rat to death. The rat has sharp teeth and sharp claws. What would happen if the snake tried to eat the rat while it was alive?

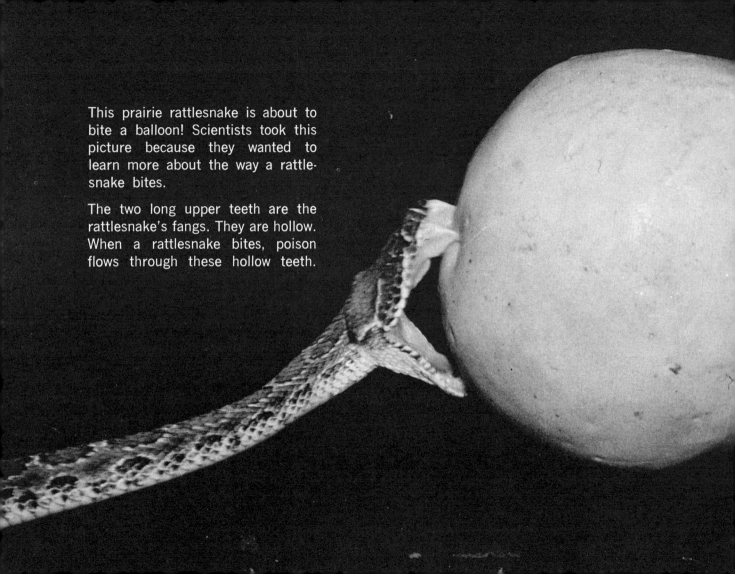

This prairie rattlesnake is about to bite a balloon! Scientists took this picture because they wanted to learn more about the way a rattlesnake bites.

The two long upper teeth are the rattlesnake's fangs. They are hollow. When a rattlesnake bites, poison flows through these hollow teeth.

Enemies

Snakes have a lot of enemies. Hogs kill snakes. Skunks kill snakes. So do raccoons and bears and hawks and crocodiles. These animals — and others too — are always ready to kill snakes and eat them.

Most people do not eat snakes, but people often try to kill snakes. So people are also enemies.

How do snakes keep from being killed? What do they do when an enemy is near?

Most of the time, snakes run away and hide. They hurry into the nearest hole. They slide under the nearest rock. Or they keep moving until they are far away from the enemy.

Sometimes a snake does not move at all when it is in danger. If a snake does not move, the enemy may not see it.

Some snakes have other ways to keep from being killed and eaten. Here are some of the things they do.

☐ Some snakes make a bad smell when they are annoyed. Garter snakes do this, and so do many other kinds of snakes. The smell is so bad that most enemies go away quickly.

☐ Some snakes curl up in a ball. They hide their heads inside the ball.

A green snake is hard to see when it is in a bush. It looks like part of the bush.

This rubber boa is curled in a ball, with its head at the bottom and its tail at the top.

An enemy will probably leave this snake alone. A curled-up snake is hard to eat! But if the enemy does take a bite, it will bite the boa's tail. And that won't hurt the boa at all.

☐ Some harmless snakes act just like dangerous snakes.

A hog-nose snake is a harmless snake. But when an enemy comes close, the hog-nose snake puffs itself up and flattens its head and neck. It jabs at the enemy with its big, flat head. And it makes a loud noise — *hissss! hissssss!*

Sometimes this is enough to scare the enemy away.

What if the enemy doesn't go away? Then the hog-nose snake tries something else. It plays dead!

☐ Some snakes shake their tails when they are in danger. If the snake is crawling through crisp dry leaves, the shaking makes a noise. The noise scares some enemies away.

Timber rattlesnake

A rattlesnake's rattle is something like a string of beads. It is made of bony rings, one next to the other.

When the rattlesnake shakes its tail, the rings jiggle against each other and make a noise.

A rattlesnake can make that same kind of noise with its tail no matter where it is crawling. It has a *rattle* on its tail.

If you whisper CH-CH-CH-CH-CH very fast, it will sound something like a rattlesnake shaking its tail.

A rattlesnake shakes its tail only when it is in danger. It never shakes its tail when it is about to catch an animal for dinner. That would scare the animal away.

If nothing else works, the snake may fight the enemy.

A snake fights the only way it can. It *bites*. Some snakes that are not poisonous can give you a nasty bite.

A person who is bitten by a poisonous snake may get very sick, or may even die.

Moving Around

One of the hardest things to understand about snakes is how they move.

Snakes do not have feet and legs. But a snake has strong muscles all along its body. It uses its muscles when it moves.

Just for a minute, do not think about snakes. Think about your feet. Move your feet inside your shoes. Wiggle your toes. When you do that, you are using the muscles of your feet.

Now take off one shoe and let your foot rest on the floor. Try to make your foot move along the floor by wiggling your toes. Even if your foot does not move very far, you will get some idea of how a snake moves. Its muscles do all the work.

Most of the time, a snake moves in a wavy line. It pushes its body — first one side, then the other — against pebbles and plants and other things on the ground. A snake cannot move this way if the ground is smooth and flat.

On smooth, flat ground, a snake moves in a straight line. It pushes some of its muscles down against the ground to do this.

A snake that is moving in a wavy line can move faster than a snake that is moving in a straight line. But no snake is *really* fast. If you had a race with a snake, you would win.

Keeping Warm

A snake can make itself warm by lying in the sun.

It can make itself warm by lying on a warm rock.

It can make itself warm by lying on the warm ground.

But a snake cannot get warm when it does not have a warm place to lie. A snake gets cold when everything around it is cold.

Snakes usually have to warm themselves after they wake up every day. Getting warm takes a while.

As soon as a snake is warm, it can start moving around. It can hardly move when it is cold. It cannot look for food, or keep itself safe from its enemies.

This snake is warming itself on a warm rock. Soon it will be ready to start the day.

A snake will freeze to death when everything around it is three or four degrees below freezing. So you will not see any snakes moving around outdoors in snowy, icy weather.

By the time winter comes, all the snakes have gone to a warmer place. They have crawled into caves or piles of rocks or holes deep in the ground. They will lie there without moving until the weather is warm again.

When a snake spends the winter this way, we say that it is *hibernating*.

These copperheads have been hibernating together all winter.

Do snakes sleep when they are hibernating? No. But when a snake is not hibernating, it sleeps every day. A snake sleeps with its eyes open. (It can't close them!)

Scientists used to think that snakes had no way at all to get warm. Whenever they touched a snake in the laboratory, the snake felt cold to them. So they thought that snakes were always cold.

The scientists didn't know that their snakes felt cold because their laboratories were cold!

Later, other scientists studied snakes more carefully. These scientists tried keeping snakes in a *warm* room. After the snakes were in a warm room for a while, the scientists touched them. The snakes felt warm.

That is how the scientists found out that a snake's body gets cold when the snake is in a cold place, and warm when the snake is in a warm place. This is what we mean when we say that a snake is *cold-blooded*.

Pictures of Snakes

When you turn the page, you will find photographs of 23 different snakes.

You will be able to see most of these snakes in a zoo. You may also be able to see some snakes right where you live.

Snakes can be found in all kinds of places.

Some snakes live near creeks and streams. Some live in the mountains. Some live in sandy deserts, and some live in muddy swamps.

Some snakes live in fields and on farms. Some live in the woods.

And some snakes even live in big cities. If you live in a city, maybe you will find some snakes in a park or in an empty lot.

You may have to look hard, though. Some snakes do not come out until it is dark. And all snakes are shy. They hide under logs and stones, and they hide in holes.

If you live in a place where there are poisonous snakes, you must be careful when you look for snakes. Always wear high leather shoes. Never stick your hand under a log or into a pile of stones. And do not look for snakes unless you go with somebody who knows how to do it safely.

When you see a real snake, will it look like its photograph? It probably will, but its colors may be different.

Some snakes (not poisonous)
that live in the United States
and Canada

Hog-nose snake A hog-nose snake has a turned-up snout. The snout helps it dig for toads — one of its favorite foods.

A hog-nose snake puts on a big show when it is in danger. (See page 29.) It will not put on a show, though, after it has lived in a zoo for a while.

Hog-nose snakes live in the central and eastern parts of the United States and along parts of the Canadian border. They are about two feet long, and they have fat, dark bodies.

They look something like some poisonous snakes of the United States. So people sometimes kill them, even though they are harmless.

Red-bellied snake A red-bellied snake is only as big as a worm when it is born — about two inches long. When it is grown, it is 10 or 12 inches long. It eats insects and worms.

Red-bellied snakes live in the eastern half of the United States and the southeastern part of Canada. The snake in this picture is lying on its back, with its red belly showing.

39

Indigo snake When an indigo snake comes out of its egg, it is about two feet long. When it is grown, it is seven or eight feet long — longer than your bed. It is longer than any other kind of snake in the United States.

Indigo snakes are dark blue or black or brown. They live in the southeastern part of the United States.

An indigo snake is not fussy about its food. It eats mice and rats and birds and lizards and frogs. It also eats other snakes.

Some people keep indigo snakes as pets.

Whipsnake You wouldn't want a whipsnake for a pet. It is not poisonous, but it has a nasty temper. When it is caught, it usually bites.

Whipsnakes live in the southern half of the United States, from coast to coast. Some whipsnakes also live in Washington State and Oregon.

All whipsnakes are long and thin. Most are three to five feet long, but one kind — the coachwhip — is often longer. (The snake in the picture is a coachwhip.) Whipsnakes eat mice and birds and snakes and lizards.

A whipsnake moves fast when it is in danger — faster than almost any other snake in the country. Another snake, the racer, is just a little faster.

Rubber boa The rubber boa is one of the slowest snakes in the country. It would probably take a rubber boa about five hours to crawl one mile.

You can find rubber boas along the West Coast of the United States and Canada. They are short, fat snakes — about two feet long. They eat small mice and rats, lizards, birds, and insects.

Rubber boas never try to bite. When they are in danger, they curl up in a ball. (See pages 28 and 29.)

Ring-neck snake　Some ring-neck snakes twist their tails when they are in danger. When a ring-neck snake does this, its bright underside can be seen—bright red or orange or yellow.

Maybe these bright colors help to scare some enemies away.

Most ring-neck snakes also have a bright ring of orange or yellow just below the head.

Ring-neck snakes are found in nearly every state and in parts of Canada. They are about 15 or 20 inches long. Mostly they eat small salamanders. They also eat worms, small snakes, lizards, and frogs.

Garter snake Every state in the United States has at least one kind of garter snake. Some kinds of garter snakes live in Canada too.

Most garter snakes have one or two or three yellow stripes down the back, with dark spots in between. Most are two or three feet long, but some are nearly five feet long.

If you had a five-foot garter snake in your bathtub, the snake would reach from one end of the tub to the other.

Many garter snakes live near streams and creeks and rivers. They often eat frogs and toads and fish — animals that they find in or near the water. When a garter snake is caught, it usually bites.

Water snake Water snakes are related to garter snakes. They are never far from water.

Sometimes water snakes lie on branches over the water, sunning themselves. When they want something to eat, they dive into the water and get a turtle or a fish or some frogs or toads.

They also dive into the water when they are in danger.

Like garter snakes, water snakes often bite when they are caught.

Most water snakes live in the eastern and southeastern parts of the United States, and some live in Canada. They are about three or four feet long, and their bodies are thick.

Rainbow snake   This snake is sometimes called a mud snake. It is usually found deep down in some muddy, swampy place in the southeastern part of the United States.

Rainbow snakes eat eels, fish, salamanders, and frogs. They are about four feet long, and they have sharp, pointed tails.

Some people think a rainbow snake can sting with its tail. Some think it can put its tail in its mouth and roll like a hoop. But no snake can do these things!

Green snake   Green snakes live mostly in the eastern United States and in southeastern Canada. They eat caterpillars and spiders.

Rough green snakes (the kind in the picture) are often found in trees and bushes. They are about two feet long. *Smooth* green snakes are about 15 inches long and are often found in gardens.

A green snake is so green and so thin that it is often hard to see. If you are lucky, maybe you will find one. It is as harmless as it looks.

47

Bull snake A bull snake is a harmless snake that doesn't *act* harmless. It will jab its head at you, shake its tail, and hiss loudly. But it is only putting on a show.

Bull snakes live in many states and in a few parts of Canada. They are usually about five feet long.

In some places, bull snakes are called pine snakes or gopher snakes. Farmers are glad to have them around, because they eat the rats and mice that live in fields and farm buildings.

48

Rat snake   There are a lot of different kinds of rat snakes. Some are called rat snakes, some are called chicken snakes, and some are called corn snakes.

They got these names because they eat rats and chickens, and because they are sometimes found in cornfields.

Farmers like rat snakes when they eat rats and mice, but not when they eat chickens or chicken eggs.

Rat snakes live in almost every part of the United States. Some live in the southern part of Canada. They are usually three or four feet long, and most are good at climbing trees.

The picture shows a yellow rat snake.

King snake Almost every state has at least one kind of king snake. King snakes also live in southeastern Canada.

Some king snakes have stripes. Some have spots. Some have colored rings around their bodies. And some are all one color.

Some live in the desert, some live in the mountains, and some live in the woods. The king snake in the picture lives in the eastern part of the United States. It is usually three or four feet long.

King snakes often eat other snakes. They will even eat rattlesnakes. A rattlesnake's poison will not hurt a king snake.

Milk snake A milk snake is a kind of king snake. Milk snakes live in most parts of the United States and in the southeastern part of Canada. Most are two or three feet long.

Milk snakes are often found on farms and in barns. They got their name because farmers used to think they took milk from the cows.

Whenever the cows didn't give enough milk, the farmers blamed the snakes.

But milk snakes do not drink milk. Then what are they doing around a farm? They are looking for mice and rats to eat. Without knowing it, they are really doing the farmers a favor.

51

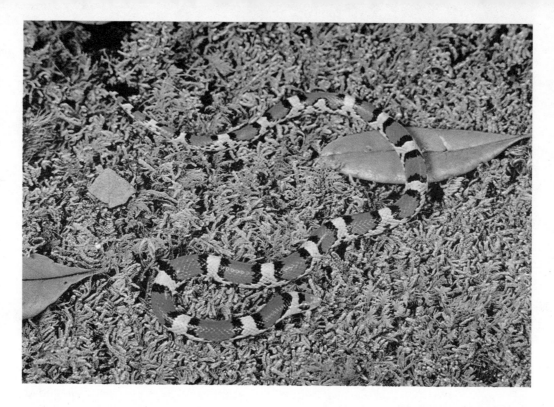

Scarlet snake   Scarlet snakes are about 15 or 20 inches long. They live in the southeastern part of the United States. During the day, they stay hidden. At night they come out and look for food.

Scarlet snakes eat small animals — small mice, small lizards, small snakes. They also eat snake eggs and turtle eggs.

A scarlet snake is red, yellow, and black. It is harmless, but it looks something like the poisonous coral snake.

Coral snake There are two kinds of coral snakes in the United States.

They both have black snouts. They both have black, red, and yellow (or white) rings around their bodies. They both eat snakes and lizards. And they are both poisonous.

One kind — the kind in the picture — is usually two or three feet long. It lives in Alabama, Arkansas, Florida, Georgia, Louisiana, Mississippi, North and South Carolina, and Texas.

The other kind lives in Arizona and New Mexico. It is about a foot and a half long.

Coral snakes do not live in Canada.

53

Rattlesnake There are 26 different kinds of rattlesnakes in the United States. Most kinds live in the Southwest. But every state except Maine has at least one kind of rattlesnake. Canada has some rattlesnakes too.

All rattlesnakes have pits and rattles. (See pages 22 and 30.) They all have long fangs. (See page 24.) And they all have heads shaped like triangles.

Mostly they eat mice and rats and rabbits.

The biggest and most dangerous rattlesnake of all is the diamondback — the kind in the picture.

Diamondbacks sometimes grow to be five or six feet long, or even longer. The longest one ever found was eight feet long. (A very tall basketball player is about seven feet tall.)

Copperhead Copperhead snakes have pits and fangs, and their heads are shaped like triangles. They do not have rattles.

Copperheads are about two and a half feet long, and sometimes longer. They eat mice and snakes and lizards and large insects.

They can be found in most parts of the eastern half of the United States, from Texas to Massachusetts. There are no copperheads in Canada.

Cottonmouth A cottonmouth has pits and fangs, and its head is shaped like a triangle. When it is excited, it opens its mouth wide. The inside of its mouth looks like white cotton.

Sometimes it is hard to tell the difference between a cottonmouth and a water snake (page 45). Both live in swampy or watery places, both are three or four feet long, and both have thick bodies.

Cottonmouths eat fish, frogs, snakes, lizards, small turtles, baby alligators, and birds. They live in Alabama, Arkansas, Florida, Georgia, Illinois, Kansas, Kentucky, Louisiana, Mississippi, Missouri, North and South Carolina, Oklahoma, Tennessee, Texas, and in southeastern Virginia.

They do not live in Canada.

Boa constrictor   Boa constrictors live in warm places — Mexico, Central America, and parts of South America. They live in jungles and forests.

A new-born boa constrictor is about 20 inches long — not quite as long as your mother's arm. When it is grown it will be about 10 feet long. The longest boa ever found was 18½ feet long — as long as a big car.

Boa constrictors kill their food by constricting it. That is, they squeeze it to death. (See page 24.)

Here are some of the animals they have killed and eaten: rats, birds, lizards, ducks, and rabbits.

Anaconda Anacondas live in South America and on the island of Trinidad. They are sometimes called water boas because they spend most of their time in the water.

Anacondas eat alligators, turtles, and fish. They also eat ducks, deer, and sheep. They kill their food by squeezing it to death.

Grown anacondas are often 25 feet long — longer than four tall people lying in a straight line.

Some men once found an anaconda that was longer than *six* tall people. It was 37½ feet long. At least, that's what the men said when they found it.

If the men were right, the anaconda is the biggest snake in the world. But scientists are not sure that the men were right.

Python Some pythons are small, but most kinds are very big. The biggest kind of all is the *reticulate* python, the kind in the picture. Some men once found a reticulate python that was 33 feet long — as long as a big bus.

Reticulate pythons and some other pythons live in Asia. Other pythons live in Africa.

All the big pythons eat big animals — animals such as sheep, goats, and pigs. They kill their food by squeezing it to death.

Cobra Most cobras are four or five feet long. Some live in Africa, and some live in India and other parts of Asia. They are all poisonous.

When a cobra is excited, it rears up and makes its neck big and flat. That is called spreading its hood. Then it may hiss and try to bite.

The Indian cobra (the kind in the picture) can make its neck bigger than any other kind of cobra. It is often found in the villages of India, where it finds rats and mice to eat. It also eats small birds and frogs.

Index

A page number printed in color means there is a photograph on that page.

Common and scientific names

Every snake has two different names — a common, everyday name that most people use, and a Latin name that scientists use. Here are the names of the 23 snakes in the color photographs.

Anaconda, *Eunectes murinus*, 58

Boa constrictor, *Boa constrictor*, 57
Bull snake, *Pituophis melanoleucus*, 48

Coachwhip, *Masticophis flagellum*, 41
Cobra
   Indian cobra, *Naja naja*, 60
Copperhead, *Agkistrodon contortrix*, 55
Coral snake
   Eastern coral snake, *Micrurus fulvius*, 53
Cottonmouth, *Agkistrodon piscivorus*, 56

Garter snake
   Eastern garter snake, *Thamnophis sirtalis sirtalis*, 44
Green snake
   Rough green snake, *Opheodrys aestivus*, 47

Hog-nose snake, *Heterodon platyrhinos*, 38

Indigo snake, *Drymarchon corais couperi*, 40

King snake, *Lampropeltis getulus*, 50

Milk snake
   Eastern milk snake, *Lampropeltis triangulum triangulum*, 51

Python
   Reticulate python, *Python reticulatus*, 59

Rainbow snake, *Farancia erytrogramma*, 46
Rat snake
   Yellow rat snake, *Elaphe obsoleta quadrivittata*, 49
Rattlesnake
   Eastern diamondback rattlesnake, *Crotalus adamanteus*, 54
Red-bellied snake, *Storeria occipitomaculata*, 39
Ring-neck snake
   Western ring-neck snake, *Diadophis punctatus amabilis*, 43
Rubber boa, *Charina bottae*, 42

Scarlet snake, *Cemophora coccinea*, 52

Water snake, *Natrix sipedon*, 45

If you are very interested in snakes, you may want to be a *herpetologist* some day.

Herpetologists are scientists who study reptiles (snakes, alligators, crocodiles, turtles, and lizards) and amphibians (salamanders, toads, and frogs).